GRACEFULLY WAITING

ISBN-10: 978-1-7350143-1-9

Publisher and Editor:

Fiery Beacon Publishing House

(Fiery Beacon Consulting and Publishing Group)

Greensboro, N.C.

Literary Consultant: Alyshia Taylor, Taylor Publishing Group

Printed in the United States of America.

Gracefully

Waiting

By

Kierra Jones

TABLE OF CONTENTS

ACKNOWLEDGEMENTS

I would like to thank God, for giving me the gift of writing and for using me to encourage others. I would like to thank my support system.

DEDICATION

This book is dedicated to all the beautiful women who
are waiting. God has good plans for you. Delight in him
and trust him to order your steps. He will never leave you
or let you down. I love you all.

INTRODUCTION

Waiting is something this generation of people does not like to do. I know I do not like it either. I feel like I am always in a rush to get to the next destination. I feel as if I need to know what happens next to better plan for possible curveballs. Wouldn't it be ideal if we had a blueprint for our lives? I mean, it would make things so much easier if we could just see every situation or plot designed to make us cry or fail. It would be easier if we can just have what we want when we want it Right? Wrong! We must trust God, and His plans for us. His plans are good. (Jeremiah 29:11) The promises of God are YES and Amen! Every time we read His word; it is a promise. Sometimes the promise, happens instantly. More often than not, we have to **WAIT**. What has God promised you? What are you believing Him for? Do you have the faith to believe that He can, and he will, or are you just saying that you trust God, while doing things your own way and finding yourself in continuous cycles ending nowhere?

Waiting is imperative for proper growth and development. God makes everything beautiful in time. The bible instructs us to "Wait on the Lord and be of good cheer and He will strengthen thine heart." What are you thinking about, while you are waiting? What is your heart's posture? Are you complaining all the time about your life? Are you serving with an attitude of thanksgiving? God desires to give us good things. He wants the absolute best for us.

It is important to understand that you are not alone in your waiting.

Sarah waited for God's promise to be performed in her life.

Hannah waited as she prayed earnestly for a son.

Ruth waited for her Boaz.

Esther waited to be redeemed.

LOVE YOURSELF

Do you like being by yourself? Are you comfortable in your own skin? Do you treat yourself well? Are you constantly seeking validation from others? If you answered NO to any of these questions you need to practice loving yourself.

Sis, you must learn to love yourself first. You are made in the image and likeness of God. You are fearfully and wonderfully made. Now, you will not learn this overnight. This takes time. As a daughter of the king, you are royalty. You should act accordingly.

How you treat yourself sets the tone for how others will treat you.

1 Cor. 13:13

Psalms 139:14

1 John 4:7

How can I love myself more?

_____

_____

_____

_____

_____

_____

_____

_____

_____

_____

_____

_____

_____

_____

_____

_____

_____

_____

_____

BITTERNESS

Are you bitter, while you are waiting? Are you angry at exes? Are you jealous of people who seem to have everything you are waiting for? Well, you must not have any of that negative stuff in your heart. God cannot bless mess. Sis, if you are harboring UN forgiveness in your heart then you are a mess. Trust me I understand, how it seems as if everyone is getting blessed before you. I know what it feels like to have God speak to you concerning certain situations, and it feels like it is not coming to pass but guess what sis? You have to keep trusting God. Ask Him to work on your heart. Do not allow yourself to become bitter.

Hebrews 12:15

Ephesians 4:31

Proverbs 14:10

Pretty Lady, don't be bitter!

_____

_____

_____

_____

_____

_____

_____

_____

_____

_____

_____

_____

_____

_____

_____

_____

_____

_____

_____

_____

_____

_____

PATIENCE

PATIENCE. While you are waiting, you cannot be overly anxious or impatient. (Phil. 4:6) You have to wait patiently. You have to believe that God, is going to do what he promised you. For he is indeed faithful. He is a man that cannot lie.

"The testing of your faith produces patience, and let patience have her perfect work." James 1:3-4 Waiting is difficult, I know. It seems like everyone is getting their blessings from God, but you. However, if God said it. It will come to pass.

Other Scriptures on Patience:

-Deut.3:16

-Phil. 1:6

-Eccl. 7:8

Let's talk about it! Am I being patient, or am I trying to help God out?

_____

_____

_____

_____

_____

_____

_____

_____

_____

_____

_____

_____

_____

_____

_____

_____

_____

COMPARISON

Sis, why are you worrying about how someone else looks, dresses, or her happiness? Why are you not an active part of your own destiny? Don't you realize how beautiful you are? Don't you realize that you are an amazingly unique individual and that there is not anyone on this planet like you? Do those things that set your soul on fire. Walk in your purpose. Stay in your lane.

2 Cor. 10:12

Galatians 1:10

Phil. 2:3

1 Cor. 4:7

Exodus 20:17

Sis, you are bad! Don't compare yourself to anyone.

_____

_____

_____

_____

_____

_____

_____

_____

_____

_____

_____

_____

_____

_____

_____

_____

_____

_____

_____

_____

_____

PERCEPTION

How you choose to view different situations and circumstances, changes everything. Do you see the glass as being half empty or half full? Things are not always as they appear. It is the enemy's job to make you feel as if you are the only one waiting, the only one going through.

Eccl. 2:14

Sis, remain positive! Life is good, but God is BETTER!

_____

_____

_____

_____

_____

_____

_____

_____

_____

_____

_____

_____

_____

_____

_____

_____

_____

_____

Celibacy

In this modern sexualized society, the concept of practicing abstinence is foreign. So, to be perfectly honest, I thought being a virgin was so weird. I thought that it was going to be "Easy" because NO ONE desired me. No one thought that I was pretty enough to be their girlfriend.

"Let's Talk about Sex baby, let's talk about you and me!"

No matter your age, you face temptation from being constantly challenged to working in a high-performance environment, it exists all around us. Let's say you give in to temptation. Now what?

What happens after sex? Both individuals go back to their lives, and if emptiness was a factor, the status is more prevalent when the high dissipates. Sex was God's idea. He designed it to be between two married individuals. When you sleep with individuals you are not married with, you become one with them. This creates soul ties. Soul ties are dangerous. You take on the other individual(s) spirits.

1 Cor. 7:8

1 Cor.6:19

Sis, the struggle is REAL!

Idolatry

I know that sometimes, it feels as if you are the only one walking through your journey, going out to dinner, movies, or even vacations alone. It seems as if everyone you know is booed up. Are you making your desire to be married or in a happy relationship an idol? If you are doing this, you are making it a God, and you shall have no other Gods before our Savior.

Lev. 26:1

Exodus 20:3-6

Sis, are you making marriage a god?

_____

_____

_____

_____

_____

_____

_____

_____

_____

_____

_____

_____

_____

_____

_____

_____

_____

_____

_____

_____

_____

_____

Find Joy in the JOURNEY

Don't be discouraged. God causes all things to work together for the good of them who love the lord and are called according to his purpose. (Romans 8:28)

-Galatians 6:9

-Joshua 1:9

-Isaiah 40:31

You have to say it until you see it. Faith without works is completely dead.

Don't worry! Be HAPPY!

PRAYER

Sis, Let's Pray Together.

Father,

I thank you for being a good, good Father. Thank You for Your unconditional love. Thank You for ordering my steps. Teach me how to wait on You. Help me to Trust Your plans for my life. Help me not to despise the process. Everything happens when You say that they do. Help me to surrender my will for Yours. Help me to be a light to the world. I am Your daughter; let Your will be done in my life. I thank You, because You do all things well. I thank You for the victory. In Jesus name, Amen.

CONNECT WITH THE AUTHOR

Kierra Jones is a native of Greenville, North Carolina. a
graduate of Gates County High School (2006.) Along
with many accomplishments Kierra holds a degree in
Culinary Arts, obtained from College of the Albemarle in
2009 located in Elizabeth City, North Carolina. She enjoys
writing, cooking, and traveling. Kierra's vision is
to encourage women to trust God.

Made in the USA
Columbia, SC
24 July 2020